The local mystery of
ROBIN HOOD

Clive Whichelow

Published by

Enigma Publishing
4 Charnwood Avenue
London SW19 3EJ
www.enigmapublishing.co.uk

First edition September 2000

ISBN 0 9524297 2 1

By the same author:
Mysterious Wimbledon (with Ruth Murphy) ISBN 0 9524297 0 5
More Mysterious Wimbledon (with Ruth Murphy) ISBN 0 9524297 5 6
Pubs of Wimbledon Village (Past & Present) ISBN 0 9524297 1 3
Secrets of Wimbledon Common & Putney Heath ISBN 0 9524297 6 4

Printed by Roebuck Press

CONTENTS

LOCAL PLACES NAMED AFTER ROBIN HOOD (not to scale)

LEGEND

1 Original Inn
2 Present pub
3 Original church
4 Present church
5 Original schoolhouse
6 Present school
7 Robin Hood gate
8 Original farmhouse
9 RobinWood farm
10 Robin Hood well
11 Robin Hill
12 Sherwood Lodge
13 Robyn Hoode Walke
14 KLG building
15 Robin Wood Close

INTRODUCTION

Walking around Wimbledon, Kingston, and Richmond Park one is struck by the number of references to Robin Hood. But why here, so far from Nottingham and Sherwood Forest? Is it simply a case of Robin Hood being a popular name or is there more to it?

Today we have Robin Hood Way, the Robin Hood public house, Robin Hood Gate at Richmond Park, etc., and in previous years there have been many other local names connected with the outlaw.

But perhaps the most surprising fact is that the first local place named after Robin Hood occurs *a hundred and fifty years* before any place being named after him in Sherwood Forest.

Robyn Hoode Walke existed in what is now Richmond Park as far back as the reign of Henry VIII, i.e. at the time when the Robin Hood legend was really beginning to capture the public imagination.

So what is the story behind the local mystery of Robin Hood, and why has it taken such a hold here?

Kingston Vale Church.

'ROBIN HOOD' CHURCH (St. JOHN THE BAPTIST) c.1925

WHO WAS ROBIN HOOD?

After centuries of research, even now going on more intensively than ever before, no one knows for certain exactly who Robin Hood was – if he ever existed at all.

Various theories have been put forward such as that of Joseph Hunter in 1852 who concluded that he was the Robyn Hode in the service of Edward II around 1324, who had previously been a supporter of anti-royalist Earl Thomas of Lancaster. After Lancaster's defeat at the battle of Boroughbridge in 1322 Hode became an outlaw in Barnsdale, was later pardoned by the king, and became his valet.

The strongest contender currently for the original outlaw is one Robert Hod who escaped justice at the York King's assizes in 1225, and was mentioned several times in the pipe rolls. This individual has been purported to be Robert of Wetherby, an outlaw hunted by the Sheriff of Yorkshire (perhaps also known as Sheriff of Nottingham) and hanged in 1225.

But scholars and historians have also found that Robin Hood, and similar names were not uncommon in Mediaeval England, and that the name was also used as a nickname, or alias as early as 1262, and as far afield as Berkshire.

So it seems that whether or not a real Robin Hood outlaw ever existed the legend had already begun to take on a life of its own at a very early stage and any 'real' Robin Hood would have been lost in the embellishments to his story.

The first literary reference to Robin Hood came in 1377 in William Langland's *Vision of William Concerning Piers Plowman*:

If I shulde deye bi this day me liste noughte to loke;
I can noughte perfitly my pater-noster as the prest it syngeth
But I can Rymes of Robyn Hood and Randolf Earl of Chestre
Ac neither of owre lorde ne of owre lady the leste that evere was made

The gist of which is:

I do not know my paternoster perfectly as the priest sings it
But I know rhymes of Robin Hood and Randolph, Earl of Chester

It is here that the legend really begins. Scattered references to Robin Hood can be found in the early 15th century which generally seem to be critical of the outlaw legend, decrying the fact that people prefer listening to tales or songs of Robin Hood than attending mass. So it seems that even at this early date the legend had wide popularity.

The first record of a Robin Hood play is in 1426 when the city of Exeter paid 20d for the privilege of a performance.

Over the next century Robin Hood became firmly established as a folk hero, and if he had ever existed at all then the legend was probably already well beyond historical truth.

THE ORIGINAL SCHOOLHOUSE (SCHOOLROOM WAS IN FAR LEFT PART OF BUILDING)

By the middle of the 13th century the name Robyn Hood or Robehod also seems to have become a generic term for an outlaw and it is probably this that helped blur the line between fact and fiction.

By the start of the 15th century the first poem about the outlaw had appeared, and it is believed that around the same time the *Gest of Robyn Hode* was assembled from several earlier tales. This 13,900-word work has been published in various forms over the centuries and continues to be the subject of much scholarly interest and interpretation.

In the 16th century Robin Hood had become a regular character in the May Games, and it is at this point that he began to take root in our local place names.

Robin Hood and the Shepheard :

Shewing,
How *Robin Hood*, Little *John*, and the Shepheard fought a fore Combat.

The Shepheard fought for twenty pound, and Robin for Bottle and Bag ;
But the Shepheard ftout, gave them the rout, fo fore they could not wag.

The Tune is,   *Robin and Queen Katherine.*

ALl Gentlemen and Yeomen good,
    down adown, adown, adown,
I wish you to draw near,
    for a ftory of gallant bold Robin Hood
Unto you I will declare,
    down a, &c.
As Robin Hood walkt the Forreft along,
    down a, &c,
Some paftime for to fpie,
    there was he aware of a jolly Shepherd
That on the ground did lie,
    down a &c.
Arife, arife, cried jolly Robin,
    down a, &c.
And now come let me fee
    what is in thy bag and bottle (I fay)
Come tell it unto me,
    down a, &c.
What's that to thee thou proud fellow,
    down a, &c.
Tell me as I do ftand
    what thou haft to do with my bag and bottle,
Let me fee thy command,
    down a &c.
My fword which hangeth by my fide,
    down a &c.
Is my command I know,
    come and let me tafte of thy bottle,
Or it may breed thy woe,
    down a &c.

But the Devil a drop thou proud fellow,
    down a &c.
Of my bottle thou fhalt fee,
    until thy valour here be tried
Whether thou wilt fight or flee,
    down a &c.
What fhall we fight for cries bold Robin Hood
    down a &c,
Come tell it foon to me,
    here is twenty pounds in good Red Gold
Win it and take it thee,
    down a &c.

The Shepherd ftood all in amaze,
    down a &c.
And knew not what to fay :
    I have no money thou proud fellow
But bag and bottle fle lay,
    down a &c.
I am content thou Shepherd Swain,
    down a &c.
Fling them down on the ground,
    but it will breed thee mickle pain
To win my twenty pound,
    down a &c.
Come draw thy fword thou proud fellow,
    thou ftands too long to prate,
This hook of mine fhall let thee know
    a coward I do hate,
    Down a &c.

THE FIRST LOCAL ROBIN HOOD NAME

The first local place name connected with Robin Hood was in what is now Richmond Park.

The Park was not enclosed by Charles I until 1637, but a century before this there was a Robyn Hoode Walke at the west side of the park. The minister's accounts for the year 1541 mention this area, but unfortunately little else is given.

Intriguingly, it is one of the earliest places named after the outlaw, and appears a full *one hundred and fifty years* before any Robin Hood place name in Sherwood Forest. While this in no way hints that Robin was local to this area, it shows just how far his legend had spread in a relatively short time.

But why here? Why should a piece of land in Surrey be named after the legendary outlaw? To discover more we must look at the tradition of the Mediaeval Games in the area – and the patronage of one Henry VIII.

THE MEDIAEVAL GAMES & HENRY VIII

In the 16th century games were popular all across England and troupes of players would put on various entertainments, including the May game, the Lord of Misrule, the Hock game and the Robin Hood game. This latter game would feature displays of archery by 'Robin Hood' and his men dressed in Lincoln Green, and the characters of the play included Maid Marian, Little John, Friar Tuck, and a minstrel. Although Maid Marian and Friar Tuck had not appeared in the original tales of Robin Hood they had gradually been incorporated into the plays to become an integral part of the story.

The characters featured in the various games seem to be partly interchangeable, and one, known as the Kyngham game, features the King and Queen of May (who also feature in the May game), and The Friar. These characters can also be identified respectively with Robin Hood, Maid Marian and Friar Tuck.

The Kyngham game, although played elsewhere too, is believed to have originated in the Kingston area. Could the name simply have derived from the names of the adjoining parishes of Kingston and Ham?

But it is the Robin Hood game that concerns us here, and fortunately the churchwarden's accounts of Kingston-Upon-Thames have survived from this period and provide an invaluable record of the local festivities (original spellings are given).

Entries for 1509 and 1510 show amounts received by the church for 'Robyn Hodes Gaderyng' – three markes, and four markes respectively. Also, in 1510 some detail is shown about the expenses for the festivities:

'Pd to John Gover for Robyn Hodes cote and for Litell Jhons cote and for ye freres cote 25s, 6d'.

In 1523 there is 16d paid for the 'hyre of 20 hattes for Robin Hode', 10d for a hatte that was lost', 2d for estrygge fethers for Robyn Hode', and 2d for '2 peyre of shone for Robyn Hode and Lytell Jhon'.

Similar expenses are shown for years up to 1539. The church would pay the costs, collect the takings (gaderyngs) and use whatever profit was made for the upkeep of the church.

The festivities were held at Whitsun and at other times and were linked in with 'church ales' when the church would brew beer to be sold at the event.

The exact location of the games is not given, but one reference mentions payment for a 'killderkyn of bere drunken in the market place', while others refer to the players performing in Croydon. So if the performers were travelling around various localities it is possible that the Robyn Hoode Walke in what is now Richmond Park may have been a route to Kingston/Kingston Vale by the players prior to their performance - perhaps a procession of some sort? And this is where Henry VIII comes into the picture.

Part of what is now Richmond Park was a favourite hunting ground of the King and we also know that he was an enthusiastic supporter of the May Games. It is said that he and his courtiers would sometimes attend the May Games in disguise so they could join in the fun! So it seems that Robyn Hoode Walke appeared during the reign of Henry VIII close to a favourite hunting ground of his. Was it named in his honour, or, as some believe, by the King himself?

Whatever the case, it seems possible that there was some connection with the king, and no other explanation seems to be forthcoming for the outlaw's name to be found here. Then of course, the Robin Hood Gate into Richmond Park must have been named after the Robyn Hoode Walke – or was it?

THE MAY WINDOW

The mediaeval games at Kingston have been commemorated by a stained-glass window now in Kingston museum. The design, which was based on a 17th century window at Betley Hall in Staffordshire, depicts various characters from the Kyngham game such as the King and Queen of May and the Friar.

The Kingston window is shown on the centre pages of this book.

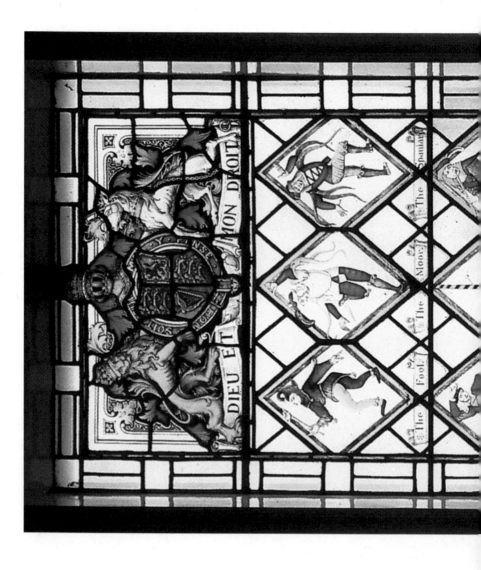

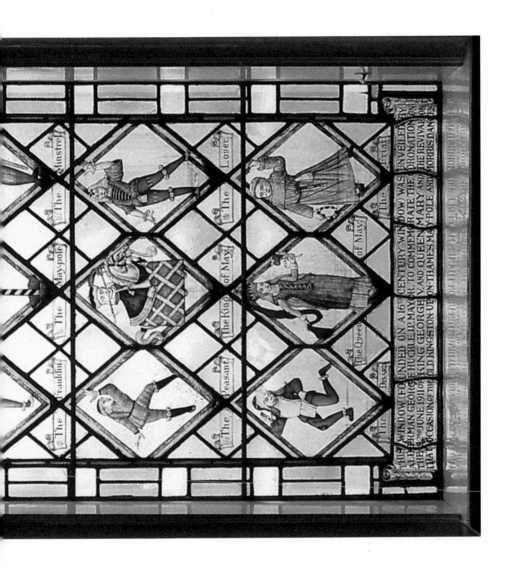

The Minstrel.

The Lover.

The Friar

The May-pole

The King of May.

of May

The Queen

The Franklin

The Peasant

The Disguisers

ROBIN HOOD GATE TODAY

ROBIN HOOD GATE

At first glance it would seem reasonable to assume that the gate was named after Robyn Hoode Walke in Richmond Park, but the gate was not named until the 1750s so why the 200 year gap?

When Charles I first enclosed Richmond Park in 1637 there were six gates, including Wimbledon Gate. This name survived for over a century and a document of 1751 still refers to it by this name. However, a map drawn in 1754 by John Eyre for George II shows it as Robin Hood Gate.

All the other gates in Richmond Park are named after the locations they lead *to* – i.e. Richmond Gate leads to Richmond, Kingston Gate to Kingston, and so on. So the inference is that Robin Hood Gate led to the Robin Hood – i.e. the inn. But why would the gate suddenly be renamed after the inn, which, as we shall see later, claims to have been there since before the park was enclosed?

Some have maintained that the inn was established in 1604, but there is circumstantial evidence to suggest that it may not have been as old as is sometimes claimed.

In 1746 cartographer John Rocque drew a map of the area as part of a survey of London and its environs. On it he showed the Halfway House Inn (later the Baldfaced Stag), and also the Fox & Coney (later the George and Dragon, and now the Kingston Lodge Hotel). He doesn't however, show the Robin Hood Inn.

All indications are therefore that the inn became established circa 1750 and that the gate was named after it. There is one objection to this, and that is: why would the gate be named after an inn which in the early 1750s had only recently been established? Who is to say that the inn would have lasted, or even kept its name?

Perhaps the most likely explanation is that the *whole area* was by now known as Robin Hood, and that it is this that the gate is named after. But why would the area be known as Robin Hood if the inn had only just appeared?

It seems the history of the inn needs closer examination.

ROBIN HOOD INN c. 1910 (NOTE SIGN AT SITE OF ORIGINAL INN READING 'EST. 1604')

ROBIN HOOD INN AND FARM

Pubs and inns have notoriously obscure histories, clouded by wild claims of antiquity, unsubstantiated legends and just plain wishful thinking. The Robin Hood is also burdened with the reflected glory of perhaps the most embroidered of all English legends. The present pub is Victorian; having been built in 1870 to replace an earlier inn which stood in what is now Robin Hood Lane.

Pictures of the present pub taken at the beginning of the 20th century show a sign nearby, at the site of the original inn across the road, reading: 'established 1604' (see picture opposite). At first this seems unlikely, as until Victorian times there was only a handful of cottages comprising the entire hamlet of Kingston Vale. There was not even a proper church here until 1861.

But the original Robin Hood inn was part of Robin Hood Farm and this had been in existence since at least the reign of Charles I.

A solicitor's report dated 1859 refers to an indenture relating to the property (the farm and the inn) dating back to the 14th of December in the 17th year of Charles I, i.e. 1642.

Intriguingly, an overseers and churchwardens' application to the Poor Law Board in 1855, requesting permission to sell the Robin Hood lands, mentions that it has been in the possession of the parish of Ham for 'upwards of 300 years'.

The Robin Hood Farm had been in a charitable trust for the benefit of the poor of the parish of Ham and Hatch since 1642, but it is possible that it existed before this.*

What is not known is when the inn began. It was not uncommon in past centuries for a tradesman to run an inn as a sideline. Carpenters and blacksmiths ran such establishments and the Robin Hood Inn may have begun its life as a sideline of the farmer's. The site of the farmhouse was once between Bowness Crescent and Keswick Avenue but that is almost half a mile from the site of the inn on the corner of Robin Hood Lane and the Portsmouth Road. Also, a legal document of 1847 refers to the farmhouse being used as an inn. However, both sites are within the extent of the farmlands so it is very possible that the inn was started by the farmer.

Whatever its origins, the inn was substantial even before the Victorian period. A builder's report circa 1830 lists: 'front and back attics, front sitting room, back bedroom, small bedroom, servants room, wc, second back bedroom, second front bedroom, public parlour, entrance hall, taproom, kitchen, scullery, cellar, yard, dairy, top bedroom, first floor bedroom, hostler's cottage and stable, wash house, coalshed and room adjoining, barn, skittle alley, and piggerys'.

---

*Note: In his *Manor of Coombe or Coombe Nevill*, Lionel Gent mentions a 1670s document, entitled *Perticulare of Come Nevill* which refers to the lease of a farm which he believes to be a predecessor of Robin Hood Farm. This was leased by a Mr Hambleton who was a butcher and grazier, though the farm does not appear to be named as Robin Hood, or indeed anything else.

ROBIN HOOD INN c. 1860 BY WICKET-GATE

It had also become a coaching inn by the 1820s, and stagecoaches such as The Rocket stopped there *en route* from London to Portsmouth. In 1821 the Rocket achieved what was then a record time for the journey – nine hours.

The inn therefore had become a relatively important and substantial establishment even before the reign of Queen Victoria and before Kingston Vale had become more than a small clutch of cottages between Wimbledon and Kingston. And regardless of when the inn itself became established, the farm/inn must have been the second place in the area named after Robin Hood. But why?

It scarcely seems likely that it was named after Robin Hoode Walke on the other side of Richmond Park. It most probably took its name from the May Games held nearby, or perhaps even *at* this venue.

And once the farm and inn were so named it seems that the small district became known as Robin Hood and it was this that prompted the name change of the Richmond Park gate in the 1750s. But the name was to spread even further over the next two hundred years.

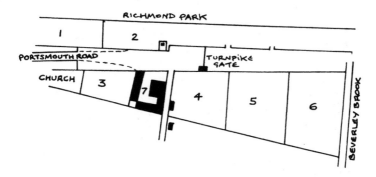

1. Meadow 2. House and garden 3. Slip of meadow 4. Meadow 5. Meadow
6. Meadow 7. Robin Hood inn.

Robin Hood inn and land (copied from a lease dated February 27th 1841)
(Not to scale)

K.L.G. Offices, Kingston Vale.

KLG BUILDING (LATER RENAMED ROBIN HOOD ENGINEERING WORKS) c. 1912

A LIFE OF ITS OWN

As mentioned previously, the tiny hamlet of Kingston Vale did not even have its own church in the early 19th century. The area was in the parish of Ham, but the Ham church was a considerable walking distance away for the locals. So in 1839 a small chapel of ease was built here. It is worth noting that when the licence was given by the Bishop of Winchester, in whose diocese it was, the area was referred to as the Robin Hood District in the Parish of Ham.

It is not known when the entire district rather than just the farm or the inn took on the name of the outlaw but the fact that it was thus called in an official church document indicates that it was, even at this stage, the accepted name.

Indeed the church, officially named St. John the Baptist, was often known as the Robin Hood church. It was replaced by a larger church nearby in 1861, and the author John Galsworthy was christened here in 1867.

By now the Robin Hood name had already begun to spread, and Caesar's Well on Wimbledon Common was known in the 18th century as Robin Hood Well. This probably came from the fact that a pathway across the common near the well was known as Robin Hood Road (i.e. the road to the Robin Hood district).

This pathway from near where Springwell Cottage now stands was shown on the John Coris map of 1787 and was probably named around the same time as the Richmond Park gate.

In 1856 the Robin Hood school was built. The building of this church school was paid for by the Duke of Cambridge, who also provided the land. The original school house is now a private dwelling, and a new school was built in Bowness Crescent in the 1950s.

In the 20th century the Robin Hood name has cropped up in the most unlikely of places.

The KLG spark plug factory, which was based in the building of the old Baldfaced Stag inn on the Portsmouth Road was known as the Robin Hood Engineering Works between 1916 and 1929. This is ironic, as the Baldfaced Stag was closed down by the Duke of Cambridge who favoured the Robin Hood inn over its nearby rival.

The name of the outlaw has also been bestowed on part of the Kingston-by-pass now known as Robin Hood Way, and there is even a Robin Hood service station nearby.

The Robin Hood name was also given to a pharmacy in Kingston Vale, a garage, and local cottages.

Other related names are Sherwood Lodge, which stood on Roehampton Vale in the 19th century and Sherwood House in Kingston Vale. There are also several Robin Wood names. A riding stables near where the old Robin Hood Farmhouse once stood is known as Robin Wood Farm and Stables. There is also a Robin Wood Place near the top of Kingston Vale.

ROBIN HOOD WELL (NOW KNOWN AS CAESAR'S WELL) c. 1910

But perhaps the most widely-known of the outlaw-related names, even if few realise its origins, is Robin Hill, the fictitious location created by John Galsworthy for the Forsyte Saga.

Galsworthy was born at Kingston Hill in 1867, and the following year the family moved to a house named Coombe Warren in what is now George Road. John Galsworthy was christened at the Robin Hood church (St. John the Baptist), and lived in the Coombe area until 1886.

When he wrote the Forsyte Saga, he based the setting for the books on the Coombe area which he knew and loved so well. He named the fictitious location Robin Hill, which was clearly inspired by the Robin Hood area nearby.

The 'Robin' names continue to interweave between fiction and real life as some of the houses near Galsworthy's old home today are named after Robin Hill.

In considering local names taken from the outlaw, perhaps not to be forgotten is the Green Man at Putney Heath. This inn may have no direct connection with the Robin Hood area but the name is often linked with the outlaw, and many Green Man inn signs depict Robin Hood as the 'Green Man'.

CHRONOLOGY

1508   The May Games, including the Robin Hood Game are held in Kingston, and possibly Kingston Vale too, from at least 1508 until 1539.

1541   Robin Hoode Walke in what is to become Richmond Park first appears in print.

1550   Robin Hood Farm may have been in existence as early as the mid 16th century, but does not seem to have taken its name from Robin Hoode walke – the link seems to have come direct from the May Games. It is now the farm/inn that gives rise to all the subsequent Robin Hood names locally.

1750   The inn, and perhaps even the district of Robin Hood, seems to have become fully established by this date.

1754   Wimbledon Gate into Richmond Park is renamed Robin Hood Gate by this date.

1787   The footpath across Wimbledon Common is named Robin Hood Road by 1787, but probably earlier, most likely around the time that Robin Hood Gate is named. Similarly, the well by the side of this road becomes Robin Hood Well about the same time.

1839   The first Robin Hood Church (officially St. John the Baptist) is built.

1856   Robin Hood School is built.

1900   Most of the other local Robin Hood names follow in the 20th century.

It seems therefore, that although Robyn Hoode Walke in Richmond Park was the first local place named after the outlaw, it did not give rise to any of the subsequent Robin Hood place names locally. This honour goes to the farm/inn which chose to adopt the name several centuries ago. And if we are surprised that a legendary folk hero had such a hold on the public imagination in those days, it is perhaps even more surprising that in these sophisticated times the legend looms as large as ever.

Robert Earl of Huntingdon
Lies under this little stone
No archer was like him so good
His wildness named him Robin Hood
Full thirteen years and something more
These northern parts he vexed sore
Such outlaws as he and his men
May England never know again!

Robin Hood's epitaph on his 'tomb' in Yorkshire

THE MODERN ROBIN HOOD SCHOOL TODAY

ACKNOWLEDGEMENTS

Ruth Murphy

Surrey Record Office

Kingston Local Studies Centre

Rosemary Haughton

Jackie Davies

Nick Redman (Whitbread)

PHOTOGRAPHS/PICTURES

Cover picture shows part of title page woodcut of Robin Hood from *Robin Hood and the Shepheard*, 1655. Reference (shelfmark) Wood 401 (13). With kind permission of the Bodleian Library, Univeristy of Oxford.

Page 10 shows full title page woodcut from above source.

Centre page photograph of May window at Kingston Museum reproduced with kind permission of Kingston Museum/Kingston Local Studies Centre.

Other pictures and photographs from author's own collection.

BIBLIOGRAPHY

Rymes of Robyn Hood – R.B. Dobson & J. Taylor

Mediaeval Games and Gaderyngs at Kingston-Upon-Thames – Dr. W.E. St. L. Finny

Palaces and Parks of Richmond and Kew – John Cloake

The Manor of Coombe or Coombe Nevill – L.E. Gent

Richmond Park – Pamela Fletcher Jones

Kingston Then and Now – Margaret Bellars